First Original Edition

Copyright© 2023 by Dwight Hairston Currence

ISBN- 979-8-9871031-4-2 (Paperback)

Published by Simply Snowden

simply
snowden

Homeless

Table of Contents

Dedication

This book is dedicated to Rev. Mark A. Evans, the pastor of Jonahville A. M. E. Zion Church. Rev. Evans fed my spirit while writing this book. Thank you, Rev. Evans, for being a great teacher of the Bible. Thank you, Rev. Evans, for being a leader of men. I will never look at homeless people the same again. I pray all who read this book feel the same.

Introduction

I wish I could tell you what inspired me to write this book. I've only been an author for three years, which has compelled me to open my eyes to things around me. I am unsure if it is being nosey or just curiosity and a desire for more knowledge and understanding. Nevertheless, I want to share the information that I have learned.

Homelessness didn't just jump out at me. I know nothing about it.

Do they have a physical identification?

Why do they keep coming back every day?

It is spooky and uncomfortable when someone walks up to me at a stoplight to ask for money or food. I think I feel this way because I don't understand. So I set out to learn more about the homeless people in my city and their story. I didn't want to feel uncomfortable or scared when they approached my car. I pray this book opens your eyes and informs you as it did for me. These are their stories.

Before sharing the stories, I googled some numbers about homelessness; 582,482 people in America are homeless. The state of California has the highest rate of homelessness in America; New York City is the city with the highest rate of homelessness in America, with Los Angles coming in second. When I think of those two cities, I have always thought of them for their glamor and wealth, but now I know that some of the poorest people live there too.

WOW, perception!

I hope this book will stimulate some thoughts and answer some of the same questions I had about homelessness.

Before we get to the stories, let's look at the people who react or judge the homeless and their perceptions.

The Egg

When thinking about "Homelessness," I start by comparing our behavior to an egg—using two parts of the egg, the outer shell and the yolk. The outer shell protects the yolk, which is an essential part of the inner core. With this in mind, I want to use four types of eggs.

The first type of egg is with a hard shell and soft yolk. That was me as a young adult before I dove into learning more about people experiencing homelessness. I would pull up to a stop light, and all I saw was a dirty man looking stinky and frightening. I would make sure I didn't look into his eyes. He had an *"I'm HOMELESS"* sign. I checked to make sure my door was locked. As he continued to walk toward me, I felt violated. I kept my focus on the light as he walked past me. The light would turn green, and I would take off. Then I would feel a sigh of relief. Now this is when the soft yolk comes into play. I didn't even get a mile away, and I felt guilty. I should have done more and would begin apologizing to the man in my mind. I thought about him sleeping outside, wondering where he would get his next meal. Pulling into my driveway, I paused momentarily and went into my house. The next day, I pulled up to a stop light, and it was a different man. I checked to make sure my door was locked, and once again, I felt violated. He walked towards me, the light turned green, and I sped off.

What is the definition of insanity?

It is doing the same thing wanting different results. Does this sound like you?

I was the egg with the hard shell and soft yolk. How about you?

The second type of egg is a soft shell and hard yolk. I was downtown talking to some homeless people when I saw a small group of people walking down the sidewalk. There was a homeless man with a sign that said, "I'm Hungry." One of the ladies began to go into her purse to get some cash. One of the guys in a nice suit said, "I got this." He reached into his pocket and gave the man $40. Not hesitating to help, the man in the suit displayed a soft shell. The homeless man thanked everyone with a smile on his face.

As the group of people walked towards me, I stopped the man with the nice suit that gave the homeless man the money. I told him I was writing a book and wanted to ask him some questions. He told everyone to continue to the office, and he would be there shortly.

This is when the hard yolk comes into play. I asked the man in the suit why he gave the man the money. You will never guess what he replied. He said, "I'm the manager of that group of people, and they follow me and watch what I do." And what he said next surprised me. He said that they should put all homeless people in jail. They are disgusting, don't want to work, and aren't veterans. I felt the chills run down my spine when he spoke. I wondered if he was married or had any kids. What would he be teaching his kids?

One word: COLDBLOODED.

Do you know someone like him?

Is that you?

Are you the egg with the soft shell and the hard yolk?

The third type of egg is with a soft shell and soft yolk. I was coming out of the market. I saw a lady talking to a homeless man. I got close enough to ear hustle. Ear hustle means to eavesdrop, to be able to hear someone else's conversation. The lady was asking him if he had a family. The man said he was from Florida, his mom died, and his brother sold the house and moved to Hawaii. The lady started telling him some words of encouragement. Our eyes met as I glanced at him, and his sad countenance ran chills down my spine. The look of pain was real, I could feel it, and I almost dropped my phone. She reached into her purse and gave him some money. He smiled and jumped up, said thank you, and ran into the store. As he got up to go into the store, he threw an empty beer bottle into the bushes. I didn't notice it until he got up. Why did the lady give him money if he had an empty beer bottle in plain sight?

Did she feel sorry for him?

Was it the look of pain in his eyes?

The lady left, and I waited on the man to come out of the store. He came out with a 12-pack of beer. He had a glow in his eyes on a mission. I tried to stop him, and he pushed me to the side and headed into the woods behind the store.

Wow! I began to process this information, not judge him. Was the pain because he needed a beer, or was it something else?

This was a prime example of wanting to stereotype homeless people.

Are you the egg with a soft shell and soft yolk?

The fourth type of egg is a hard shell and a hard yolk. I didn't actually know if I would see this type of egg. Except I did; a man had a homeless sign at the light. I saw the homeless man talking to a man in the cars ahead of me. The light turned green, and the man in the car reached out some money. When he started moving forward, the homeless man moved forward to keep up with the car. The man in the car dropped the money in the middle of the intersection. The car ahead of me stopped, and the homeless man ran to pick up the money. I could not believe what I had just witnessed. That person has a hard shell and hard yolk—one word; HEARTLESS.

I really don't want to tell you about the next but I must. I pulled up to a convenience store and saw a man outside with a sign that said, "*Vienam Vet, please help.*" I wondered if he spelled it wrong on purpose. I then began to wonder about his story. I pulled over to the air gauge to observe. I wondered if people would help him. A couple of people gave him money, and then here came this guy with a hard shell and hard yolk. He pulled right in front of the homeless guy and started talking to him before he went into the store. The guy came out of the store, leaned down to hand the homeless guy a bag, and then dropped it to the ground as he laughed at him. I wasn't able to ear hustle; I was too far away. The homeless man began to cry and started walking down the street. I was speechless, I wanted to call the cops, and I wanted to follow the guy in the car. I had to close my eyes and pray. I began to pray for the homeless guy and the man in the car. God fights all your battles.

I wondered what made the homeless guy sad to walk away, so I walked over and looked in the bag; it was a bottle of beer. I took it to the trash can and shook my head. The people with a hard shell and hard yolk are hard to deal with for me. When I see how people treat each other, I think of the lessons my grandmother taught me.

My grandmother always said these little phrases that have stuck with me. "It takes all kinds of people to make this world; always treat people how you want to be treated." There are life experiences that will make you scratch your head, but don't worry; God will handle the outcome. Now that I have you doing some thinking let's get into the meat and potatoes. I will let these people tell their stories. You can decide; drug abuse, mental illness, motherhood, or survival.

Strap-up, it's going to get real.

What type of egg are you today?

What is Homelessness?

Before we get started with their stories, let's define homelessness. I started off talking about the egg. What type of egg are you? I was several different types of those eggs before writing this book. The thought enters my mind to be a hard shell and a hard yolk; then I pray for humility.

Can you really look at a person and judge them?

Do you stereotype homeless people?

Is it because of the media or your personal experience?

How would you survive if your world came tumbling down?

What if someone stole your identity?

What if someone emptied your bank account and ran up your credit cards?

How is your mental health?

God can save people.

God can heal people.

God is the answer.

Some people need to hear it more than others.

Let's get back to the question, what is homelessness?

Homelessness, to me, is having a big hole in your heart, and it is a feeling of not being a part of anything and feeling isolated. I am sure that homelessness means many different things to different people. However, the online dictionary's meaning is the state of having no home.

Let me come from a different direction. When most people say, they go to a church, as in a church is a building, they call it a church home. To me, church means how you talk about Jesus's life with others. It doesn't matter where it is or even if it is in a building.

Now stay with me on this. Homelessness, to me, means you have no place you feel safe. Ok, here it comes. Homelessness is your safety net. The streets, the woods, and even inside your home are just a physical touch away.

You don't have to look down on people to be able to look up to yourself. You can look straight ahead. Homelessness will never go away, and this is bigger than me or you. I want to end with this thought. Do you only feel safe inside your home?

Luke 9:58 ESV

And Jesus said to him, "Foxes have holes, and birds of the air have nests, but the Son of Man has nowhere to lay his head."

James 2:15-17 ESV

If a brother or sister is poorly clothed and lacking in daily food, and one of you says to them, "Go in peace, be warmed and filled," without giving them the things needed for the body, what good is that? So also faith by itself, if it does not have works, is dead.

Their Stories

The more I see what appears to be homeless people, the more I want to know about their stories and how they got there. This man was sitting on a park bench, so I walked over, sat beside him, and said good morning. I began telling him I was writing a book on homelessness and would love to hear his story.

I'm 46 years old now. I came from a normal home with a mom and a dad living in the same house with my two older sisters, that were 3 and 4 years older than me. There was always yelling in the house. My mom was a secretary, and my dad worked at the plant. The first time I remember my dad drunk, I was about seven years old. Dad came into the house late on a Saturday night, and my mom started yelling at him because he was gone all day. He started yelling back. I didn't understand what had happened at the time. I now understand my dad began beating my mom that night. My sisters opened their door and peeked out, and I was already in the hallway trying to see what was happening. They shut their door; then I shut mine. I cried myself to sleep that night. I woke up that morning as my mom and sisters cooked breakfast, like every Sunday morning. However, that Sunday morning was burnt in my mind forever. As I said, everybody was smiling and laughing, acting as if nothing had happened the night before. My mom told Dad breakfast was ready, and he came into the kitchen smiling and laughing. When Mom sat down, there it was - my mom had a black eye. I felt sick and ate my food so fast. I went outside to walk, then started to run. I didn't know why. I didn't stop until I was out of breath. That Sunday, I no longer felt safe or protected. There were many more times of my dad's rage.

The next thing I can remember, like yesterday, was when I was 13. My oldest sister was graduating from high school. My sister came home and told my mom she was moving out. She packed her clothes and left. Mom told Dad when he came home, he flew out of the house, jumped in the car, and sped off. Dad returned in the middle of the night. I was awakened by Dad yelling and screaming. My sister peeked out of her door and then ran to my room. We held each other off to sleep.

The following week changed my life forever. One of my friends stole some of his dad's liquor. We went by the stream, and I took that first drink. It burned going down, but the feeling was priceless. I spent the next year stealing money from Mom's pocketbook, getting the change out of Dad's truck, and even stealing beer from the store. Sometimes, I could even get an older man to buy me hard liquor.

It was getting close to my other sister's graduation, and I was stressing out, knowing I would be all alone. My sister was one month away from graduating when she came home from school crying. She wouldn't tell me what was wrong, but when my mom came home, she told her that she was pregnant. As soon as my dad came home, Mom told Dad she was pregnant. Dad called my sister into the kitchen and slapped her across the room, telling her to get out of his house. My sister ran out the door, and I ran to my room and shut the door. It was time when Dad finished beating Mom, and I left.

Where did you go?

I got outside and ran as fast as I could go. I heard the horn from the train. I got a burst of energy and jumped on the train. I wedged between the ladder and the train car and held on tight. I finally got comfortable and fell asleep. I woke up, and the train was going very slow. It was going through a town, so I jumped off. I was starving and had to find something to eat. I spotted a gas station that wasn't open, but I found some fries, half a burger, and packs of mayo and pepper. For the first time since I was seven, I felt safe. The store finally opened, and I begged for money at the front of the store. I ended up with $18; I felt rich. I got a man to buy me some beer. That night was the best day of my life. I didn't know or care about *tomorrow. I stayed at the gas station for the next two weeks, and the store manager said I had to leave. I made it back to the train, and I jumped on old faithful. I spent the next ten years staying close to the train tracks.*

When I made it to this big city, I decided to stay. Not sure why, but I did. Usually, I sleep on a bench downtown, but I do make it to the men's shelter twice a year. I make anywhere from $10 to $50 a day. I steal food or beer if needed. I make sure I get my beer; I like the way it changes the way I feel. These streets are my home now, and I feel free.

Do you ever see or talk to your family?

I haven't seen my sisters, Mom, or Dad since I left. I sometimes wonder about my mom and whether my sisters got married or had any kids. Sometimes I think about reaching out, but then I remember what it was like and don't want to feel that again.

How do people on the street treat you?

People sometimes look at me with fear, and people even cross the street to avoid me.

What do you want people to know who judge you?

I've never been to jail. I don't have any kids. I've never had a girlfriend. I'm happy. I feel free.

How about you? Do you have $5? *(I gave him $20. He said thank you and walked away.)*

A free ride from myself.

As I talked to him, he hardly took a breath initially; I felt like he wanted to be heard and tell people his story. However, there was a red flag when he started talking about coming from a normal home.

Is your home normal?

Is a home normal with yelling in the house?

What is a normal family?

When I think of a normal family, I think of the TV show families, but is that realistic?

I wonder how he felt about his mom being physically abused. I think it made him stuff his feelings. I believe the alcohol began to take away the pain, making me think he ran away to keep his relationship with alcohol.

I wanted to ask him if he had ever hit a woman.

I also wanted to ask him if he would ever go back home.

I had so many more questions, but I could tell that all the talking brought back so many emotions that he didn't want to feel or deal with. He also appeared to me to be afraid of closure. I felt his not knowing about his family gave him hope. Not knowing about his sisters gave him dreams of their future. It was like make-believe. There could be a different outcome every day. I really don't believe he wanted to know. It gave him a purpose for living. I think he felt one day they would find him. He didn't say this. This is what I believe.

How did you interpret his journey?

Let me know what your thoughts are on my Facebook page D Hairston Currence

Or Instagram

https://www.instagram.com/dwighthairstoncurrence/

I saw this lady early one morning in the hospital parking lot, asking people for money. I walked up to her and asked her her story and how she got to this place.

Where do I begin?

At the beginning...

I'm 26 years old. My life changed when John told me I was pretty in the 8th grade, and I never walked past a mirror again without looking at it. This new confidence made me popular. When I first reached high school, my grades were good, and everybody wanted to be my friend. My hair was long and pretty, my mom let me wear make-up, and I also made the cheerleader squad.

My junior year in high school was when I met Zack. Zack was rebellious, a so-called 'bad boy.' He never looked my way, and I didn't understand why. One day our eyes met, and he gave me a head nod. I was so excited, and I looked for him everywhere. I saw him at lunch around his friends and then waited for him to get up. I followed him as he was leaving campus and gave him my number. I was excited that Zack called me later that day. He said there was a party this weekend if I wanted to go; I told my mom I was spending the night at one of my friends that lived on the other side of town. My mom never checked on me, so I knew I could do what I wanted.

When I got to the party at the college, there was a funny smell in the air. I soon found out that it was marijuana. I wanted to impress Zack, so I tried it. I had never felt like that before and realized I was very high. I told Zack I wanted to go home. He told me to rest for an hour and that his brother had a room upstairs. He gave me some punch and said that he would keep an eye on me, so I went to sleep on the bed.

When I woke up, most of my clothes were taken off, and Zack was nowhere to be found. I put on my clothes and ran out of the house. I found myself on the football field bleachers staring at the field, freaking out. I didn't know what had happened during the night, but I knew something wasn't right. I headed home; I knew I had at least a 3-mile walk home. I got home and took a long hot shower.

My senior year was different; I didn't know I would be on those bleachers forever. Zack never came back for our senior year and wouldn't speak to me after that night. I started skipping school and smoking pot, I didn't care about anything, and my parents didn't know what to say to me. Going to therapy was not in the headlines back then like mental illness is these days.

Anyway - I didn't have enough credits to graduate and had no plans of doing that another year. I packed a bag, and I left home. I walked to the college that changed my life and sat on the bleachers once again. I was beating myself up with thoughts of that horrific night.

As I walked to the highway, a van was at the edge of the college campus, and as I was walking by, a man got out and asked me if I wanted a ride. I said, "No," and then he asked me if I wanted to work in the next state for the weekend. He went on to say that he picks up girls for the weekend to dance, and they get $200 a night. I thought I could get far away and even get some cash, if nothing else. Two more girls were inside the van that had never been either. I got in, and then we left.

We get there, and I find out it is nude dancing. I said, "No, thank you."

The manager told me I would have to pay for the ride there if I wasn't going to dance, so I went into the dressing room with the other girls. They had pot, and that made it better. They also had cocaine, but I didn't try the cocaine, but I smoked a lot of pot. We had to dance until the early morning hours, and then they had cots for us to sleep on. At about noon, I was the first one up; I went to the bathroom and crawled out the window. I ran as fast as possible and reached a shopping center. I went into a store and stole four candy bars. They were the best candy bars I had ever eaten.

I applied for a job at a restaurant next door to be a waitress, and the manager said I could start the next day. An elementary school was around the corner, and I spent the nights in the back. The manager would let me wash up at the restaurant, and James was the cook and told me I was pretty. That took me down memory lane.

James offered to take me home, but I told him I was fine. James was nice and kept asking me to go home all week. I ended up moving in with him at the end of the week. James didn't have any pot; he had cocaine. I tried it for the first time, and I was hooked. I was spending all my money on cocaine, then James kicked me out. I knew there was only one place I could go to get cocaine, and I went back to the club. I stayed there for two years.

They took me to the hospital when I almost overdosed on cocaine, and the nurses were so nice to me. When I left, they took up a collection, and I bought myself a tent and moved into the woods behind the hospital.

The hospital is open 24 hours. It is great! I sometimes sleep in the emergency room. I hang out in the hospital parking lot and beg for money; some nurses give me clothes and money weekly. My life is great! Do you have any money to help me out? (I gave her $20. She turned and headed to the woods)

My heart goes out to her because I have daughters. I wonder if her parents have given up on her being alive. I can't even imagine carrying around that much pain. I look at the pictures in the stores that post missing children and am speechless.

Could you wake up every day and play the what if game?

How does someone with such devastating wounds heal?

I don't know how not to care. This is one of the times I put my faith in God's hands. I don't know if she was truthful or has a mental illness.

God gives me closure because he knows the truth and the outcome. I didn't get a chance to talk to her about God, but I paused and prayed for her. Thank you.

I feel safe and loved here.

I've seen this man around the University area for years, and I have never seen him beg for money. He would just sit on the bench with his buggy next to him. I went to the bench, sat beside him, and asked him what his story was.

I will tell you my story for only one reason. Maybe it will help someone else. I'm 63 years old. I grew up an only child. My mom gave me a nightlight because I was afraid of the dark. I stay up all night eating out of trash cans. My biggest fear as a child is my safest refuge today. I give new meaning to the word nightlight. My mom and dad worked at the factory. They only had a high school education, and I was my family's first to go to college. I didn't stop until I received my doctrine; I'm a psychiatrist. My ambition was to have my own practice.

My first job was at a university. My first year was exciting, and I realized my passion was teaching. I taught Psychology 101. I saw my students flourish the first year away from home, and during my second year of teaching, I felt accomplished as I could tell the ones who were determined to make it. I would walk into the classroom and see thoughts racing around their heads. I often wondered how much of your mind one controls.

It was my fourth year of teaching that my life changed forever. The university hired a new professor, and I remembered the first time I saw her. She was wearing a red dress. I couldn't get her off my mind. I didn't have a date in high school; I only had two dates in college because I focused on my future. I spent the next week trying to find her.

I didn't ask around; I didn't even know her name. We had our first staff meeting, the meet and greet for all the staff, and there she was. My mouth got immediately dry, and I could feel my heart racing. She had such a beautiful smile; I just stared at her in awe.

They had an open bar, and I noticed she wasn't drinking; we had that in common. As she moved over to the side, I got enough courage to make my move. I introduced myself to her and then asked her out on a date. I couldn't wait until Saturday to get there. We decided to meet at the backside of the library, at the lake; I packed fruit for a picnic. She showed up with her big smile and was impressed I had a plan. I felt comfortable right away, and we sat by the lake and talked for hours. She was easy to interact with, and for the first time, I admired a female. After 10 minutes of interaction, I usually got bored, but our conversation was effortless, and we lost track of time.

The following month was amazing. We had lunch dates, went on bike rides, and took long walks; needless to say, I was on cloud nine. I dropped down on one knee on our 6-month anniversary, and she said, "Yes." We bought a house around the corner from this university and walked to work together. Life was good.

Two years into our marriage, I came home to find her sitting in the kitchen with her face in her hands. I rushed to her side. She looked at me with that beautiful smile and said, "I'm pregnant." I felt like I had won the lottery. My jaws were hurting from smiling all day. I went to all the doctor's appointments. I rubbed her belly and feet daily. I even read to our unborn child.

I'm in class when I get the call; it's time. I rush home, and we head to the hospital. "It's a boy!" The feeling of holding him is beyond compare. My wife looks at me and says, "He might not be your son." I almost dropped him. I felt my whole body jerk a couple of times. I gave him to her and went into the bathroom, discombobulated. I stayed in the bathroom for two hours; I couldn't move. There's no way I can face her.

What about this sweet innocent child?

I got up, walked out of the room, and went home. I didn't sleep that night. When I returned to the hospital, I demanded a DNA test. Not resisting, the test came *back; it was my son. Now, to deal with the elephant in the room. She told me it was only one time out drinking with her girlfriends. I forgave her, but it's harder to forget. My son did make life easier to live. Time went by so fast.*

It was my son's 1st birthday. I finished up class and headed over to pick up the cake. I stopped by the florist to surprise my wife with a dozen red roses. I walked into the house and yelled, "HAPPY BIRTHDAY". There wasn't a sound. I figured they wanted to surprise me. I start looking around downstairs. Not there. I slowly started up the stairs. I get to our room. My wife was in bed with the covers over her. I pulled the covers back, and she was dead. I ran to my son's room; he was dead. I collapsed to the floor.

When I woke up, I called the police. The police arrested me. My wife had been stabbed 15 times, and my son was choked to death. They had me on suicide watch as I sat in the cell. I'm sitting in this cell on day two, and a man in a suit comes to my cell and asks me if I am ready to go home. I said, "I'm ready to go but don't have a home anymore." He took me into this room. He told me one of the students had been having an affair with my wife.

The man's eyes began to water up like it was happening to him all over again. He paused a few seconds and then continued.

His roommate brought a jacket to the police station yesterday. The roommate said he had been his roommate for three years and had been sleeping with her for three years. He said she had been to their room before. They tested the jacket; it was your wife's blood, so we brought him in this morning. He confessed to killing your wife and son. He said she told him that he was the father.

(Looking into my eyes)

Have you ever had a memory that makes your head throb, where you have to gasp for air like you are underwater?

I still see her smile. I still hear her laugh, and I still feel her touch. My son's eyes were so bright.

Gasping for air and with tears in his eyes, he got up, grabbed his buggy, and slowly walked away.

WOW!

I'm human, so don't judge me. My first thought was if he told his journey to the wrong person, it would be part of a movie.

How sick is that?

I felt his pain. Listening to him talk made me feel like I was him. I can relate to loving someone who didn't love me back. I understand why he was gasping for air. I have forgiven her and moved on, but this man's voice still quivers. His voice ran chills down my spine. My heart fluttered from his pain. I'm so grateful he talked to me. I couldn't hold back the tears as he spoke. I wanted to talk about how good God was to me, but he got up and walked away. I'm going to make some time to go back. This is only the beginning of our relationship. I can't wait to talk to him about God.

The moon is his nightlight now.

I saw this man standing outside the grocery store, I walked over to talk to him and asked his story, and he started with these demands.

> I will tell you my story for $20. You can't tell my location, and you can't describe how I look. I promise you; it will be worth $20. I can only give you 15 minutes.

I said no problem. I gave the guy $20 and checked the time on my watch.

> I have been working on this homeless game for six years. I got fired from a job. I came the following Monday and begged for money. I made $100 the first time. I realized what I had to do; it's like acting. I keep a desperate look in my eyes the whole time I play that character. It makes people dig in their pockets. I work five days a week. I usually work only 5 hours a day. I have five different locations. I get there at 7 am, and I'm headed home by noon. I have three parking lots and two stoplights. I have many people pay me once a week at the parking lots. I wait on old people pushing their carts to their cars. I help them. Mondays, I usually make $200 a day. Thursday and Friday, I make $200 - $400 a day. It's hard for me to walk away from this gravy. The way I look at it is this. Most homeless people are junkies. They take their money and buy drugs. I pay bills. I picked up an online job two years ago. It's to justify an income. I just made

$20 in 15 minutes. Your time is up. He turned and walked away.

This guy made me sick to my stomach. I got in my car. I watched him work. He preyed on older people. I watched him until noon. I followed him as he walked down the street. He parked ½ mile away. He changed his shirt, got into a 328i BMW, and drove away. I had to pray about putting this guy in this book. You deserve to know the truth. But it made me add him to my prayer list. The reason why I didn't want to put this guy in my book is because of evil. I didn't want to promote evil. Let's look at this differently; there is a battle of good versus evil in everyone. I don't believe most homeless people act like this guy.

Are some of them wanting drugs or alcohol?

I don't know. Instead of avoiding homeless people, talk to them about your life experiences. I speak to them about God; you may be the vessel to start their healing process. LOVE IS GREATER THAN EVIL.

These next three are amusement workers, the first story intrigued me, so I had to interview a couple more. Every story was different.

You can decide if they are homeless or not.

How old were you when you started with amusements?

> I'm 50 years old. I've been traveling with these rides since I was 12. My Mom got a job operating a ride in Waterbury, Connecticut, and I came along as a package deal. I grew up with this life and never met my dad.

How many different states have you been to?

> I've been to Maine, Vermont, Rhode Island, Connecticut, New Jersey, New York, Pennsylvania, Virginia, Ohio, Michigan, Indiana, Tennessee, North Carolina, South Carolina, Georgia, Alabama, Mississippi, Louisiana, Kentucky, Florida, Virgin Islands, Puerto Rico, and the Bahamas.

How long does your season last?

> We travel ten months a year and spend two months in Florida during November and December servicing the rides.

Do you feel homeless?

> I don't feel like I'm homeless. Home is where you lay your head. This is my home. I don't own a house, apartment, car, or truck. I have a bicycle. I have a room in

the living quarters. The living quarters are like mobile homes on wheels. They come along with the rides. We set up on location. Two things they give us on location are electricity and water. I rent a hotel room 4 times a year to take hot showers.

Do you see your friends and family?

I have a female friend that works one of the rides. That's her right over there. We have been dating for five years. My mom died a couple of years ago. We didn't know she had emphysema until it was too late. She smoked four packs of cigarettes a day. I only smoke one pack a day. I don't have any kids or any other family. My girlfriend can't have kids. She has two kids already. They are with her mom. She had her tubes tied. I like seeing people that I haven't seen since last year. It's almost like they are my family. They remember my name. It's cool. Sometimes every other year. They are my family when we come back around. I love traveling around to different places.

What else do you think people would want to know?

We get one free meal a day. Amusement food is good. I'm never tired of it. We pay for any more food we eat. The good thing is if I run out of money, I can take a loan. I can borrow money until the following location if I run out. We sometimes party late at night. We play cards and drink beer. We are a close family. There is only one lady that has been here longer than me. She sells tickets when we are open. My birthdays are fun. We get free funnel cakes all day. I have been to more places than most people will ever see. I enjoyed talking with you, but I must go. We must be set up tomorrow. I hope you come back next year. I will look forward to seeing you.

This next amusement worker is a young female.

When did you get started with amusements?

I'm 26 years old. I've been traveling with our team for eight years. I'm from Tawas City, Michigan. Tawas City is along Lake Huron in the lower part of Michigan. It's a small town. My parents wanted me to work in the family business. My mom is a housekeeper, and my dad is the maintenance man at the hotel. They don't even own the hotel. They have worked there all their lives. They live at the hotel for half price. The owner has Mom and Dad on call at all times. There is no way I wanted any part of that life. I'm also tired of long winters with snow and sleet. It's so funny how I got started with our team.

I had been dating Jack since high school. His friend found out they were paying people to help set up the amusement rides and tear them down. I have always been a tomboy, so I went along with them. I met most of the amusement team. They were cool and told me about all the places they traveled and what they saw. It sounded like so much fun, so I signed up, and here I am.

How many different states have you worked in?

I have been to Michigan, Pennsylvania, New York, Georgia, Florida, Texas, Louisiana, North Carolina, South Carolina, and West Virginia. We have three big warehouses in Florida. We paint the rides in January and February. We leave out in March for Georgia. We travel north up the east coast. I love the ocean. I get to hang out and get paid. It's cool. We go to New York and then head west. We circle around and always make it back to Florida in November. We set up in Jacksonville, Tallahassee, Orlando, Tampa, and Miami. Florida is so much fun in November and December. I grew up in freezing cold weather those months, so I look forward to Florida.

Do you feel like you are homeless?

I feel like a movie star. I don't feel homeless. I'm on the team with some ladies that work the games. We are family; I feel like they are my sisters. I feel free. Traveling to different places is exciting. The people are so excited to see us when we come back. I have seen children grow up before my eyes. It didn't matter when I first started. I now look forward to my relationships with them. No, I don't feel homeless. I have several homes in several states. I could stop and start a new life on any given day. Today, I'm enjoying the ride. My life is stress-free.

Are you still in touch with your family?

We make it to Michigan in June. I get to spend time with my parents. We set up in Saginaw, Michigan. It's only an hour from Tawas City, Michigan. My parents are very supportive of my life choice. My mom always cries when I leave. My dad tries to give me a gun every time I go. Growing up in the hotel was always full of strange people. Some were weird. I know I travel around and see different people every day. The difference is the people I see traveling around are happy to see me. It feels good. I feel like I bring joy and put smiles on people's faces, if only for a day. I've got to finish setting up now. I hope your book does well. Maybe you will give me a signed copy when we come back around next year. I enjoyed talking to you. It made me realize I have a great life. No, I don't feel homeless.

The last amusement worker that I interviewed was an amusement owner.

How did you get started with amusements?

My family owns a farm with 20 acres east of Arcadia, Florida. My dad quit his job and bought some kiddie amusement rides in 1962. He started just doing events in the state of Florida. After two years, He took out a second mortgage on our land.

He paid down on six adult rides. He started going to Georgia, South Carolina, and North Carolina. I was born in 1965. My mom said we all traveled with him. I have two younger sisters. I started school in 1971. Me, my mom, and my sisters stayed home. Dad had a traveling carnival by then. He came home in the winter. All the rides were in the building we had. We would help paint the rides and play on them. We had a camper; Mom pulled with the truck. We met up with Dad in the summers. I started when I was ten years old. We stopped going when I was 14, I started playing football, and we would lift weights in the summers.

When I graduated high school, I was tired of school and didn't want to work with Dad, so I joined the Marines. I didn't understand how spoiled I was. Everybody tried to tell me what to do in the Marines, and I couldn't wait to get out. It finally happened. I waited for Dad to come home in the winter and begged him to give me a job. I started at the bottom once again. I had to learn how to set up and tear down every ride all over again. It didn't feel like a job; it was fun. The best part was traveling to different places.

Where have you been with the amusement rides?

I have been to Florida, Georgia, South Carolina, North Carolina, Alabama,

Mississippi, Louisiana, Texas, Arkansas, and Virginia.

Do you feel homeless?

My mom and dad have both passed. I have two kids. My son starts school next year. My wife will stay home with my son and daughter. Arcadia, Florida, is my home for two months a year. This carnival is my home for ten months a year. I don't believe I could stay home all year. This life is in my blood. It is an adrenaline rush to set up on time and tear down to get to the next location. I have a group of people that have been with me for 20 years. We can finish each other sentences.

I believe I have rescued many people from being homeless. I hire people daily, and some of those people last a day, a month, and some a couple of years. It buys them some time to figure things out. Having a house doesn't make a home. I believe most of the drifters aren't happy. They have so much drama and confusion in their life. The problem is they don't know how to deal with it. When we have issues moving around and with each other, we work through them together. I don't believe in second chances; they know when they start. I set the rules, and you must go if you get caught stealing or having any type of drugs. There are no drugs allowed at my carnival. Too many people depend on me to keep their home safe—no second chances.

Do you miss your family?

My mom and dad passed away some time ago. I do miss my wife and kids, and I talk to them every day. I learned how to video chat. I have made a lot of money, which no longer motivates me. The lives I get to change are the gratitude that I feel. Every day I go to different places and talk about how good God has been to me.

God has saved my life. I read my Bible every morning, and my life is amazing. We will see if my kids will follow in my footsteps.

Do you feel these amusement workers are homeless?

They all seem to love traveling from place to place. I wish I had interviewed someone on a cruise ship. You can draw your conclusions. There are a lot of good people who work at the traveling amusements.

I get to this storage company at 6 am. I have a code to get into the building. I see a car parked in the corner. I go in to inspect the elevators. I start doing my paperwork from my car. The car in the corner cranks up and parks in front of the building. I see a lady get out. She has a son, and she needs to vent. I listen.

My parents told me when I was 14 that I was adopted. It was shocking. I cried most nights to sleep. I turned my focus to basketball. It took away all the pain. I earned six full scholarship offers. I chose a college, and I met this guy the first month. It was love at first sight. I didn't find out until it was too late that he was in a fraternity.

He made more time for his fraternity than me. It was fine because I played basketball for the college. In my sophomore year, I got pregnant. My parents wanted me to come back home, and I felt different knowing I was adopted. I wanted to start my own family, so we immediately moved in with his parents.

His mom smoked cigarettes in the house. It was appalling. She constantly reminded me it was her house, and I could get out if I didn't like it. My boyfriend got a job at the plant. We had enough money to get our first apartment in two months. My son had his own room. I was too sick to work. My boyfriend was complaining about me not paying my share of the bills. My relationship was sinking day by day. I moved 2000 miles away from my parents. My parents sent me money monthly to quiet his rage. My son is now ready to start school. The arguments got louder and louder. He reminded me I have no excuse not to work now. I found a job around the corner at the market.

I could put my son on the bus and be there when he left. This was when everything went south. It was the summer of my son going to the 3rd grade. There was a knock at the door. I was watching television. My son was playing his video game. It was the sheriff. My son heard the whole conversation. I was too shocked to tell him to go to the other room. We had 15 minutes to get out. There was an eviction notice put on the door last month. The sheriff let me load up my car. My boyfriend wouldn't answer the phone. I drove to the mall. I felt my own heartbeat. Do you know how you take a rag and ring it out? I had enough money to rent this storage unit.

I take my son to school every day and pick him up. I still have the same job and picked up Saturdays and Sundays. My son stays in the car. I need to go now. I was going to take my son to school. I hope my story helps someone else. Please don't put the name of this storage facility in your book. We may still be here. Thank you.

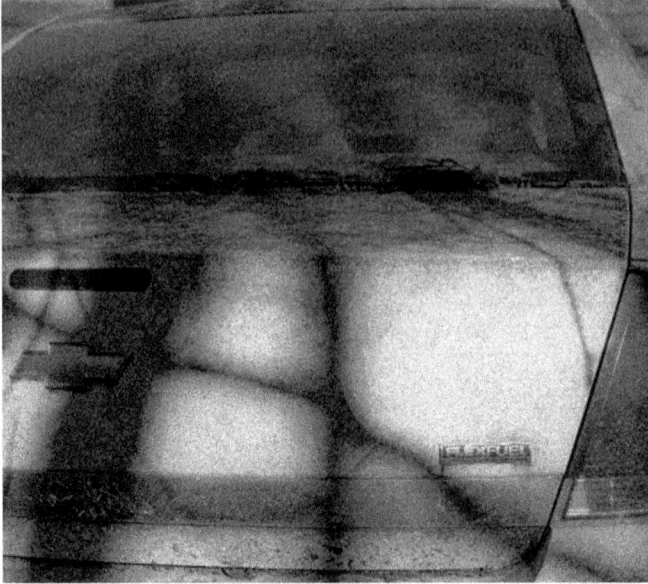

Home

I'm speechless. I will go back and check to see if they are still there. I will encourage her to go home. I will also do what I can to help.

I find my awareness has increased since I started writing this book. I would glance at people who seemed to be homeless, and now I wonder why they are homeless.

I stop to get gas first thing in the morning. I look up and see a man sitting in a chair at the edge of the woods. I would have never approached him in the past. I pumped my gas and walked over to the man. I asked him if he was homeless. He jumped out of the chair in my face and said, "Do you know who I am?"

I told him I was researching and asked if he would tell me his story.

My dad was one of the most successful doctors in this area. You see that building right there. My dad built that building. My dad built that business for me and my brother. We were groomed to follow in his footsteps. Now I have nothing. My mom never had to work a day of her life. My brother is two years older than me. He was always a suck-up. A suck-up is a tattletale. I would always get in trouble because of my brother. I never realized at the time he was protecting me. He was trying to save me. I set our dog's tail on fire, put dirt in our swimming pool, and went for a joy ride when I was 14. Do you have a cigarette? I will tell you the rest if you give me a cigarette. (I started walking towards the store. He yelled at me, "Bring me a beer." I bought him a pack of cigarettes and a beer.)

I got into a lot of trouble in school. Most of it wasn't my fault. Let me tell you about my dad. We had a million-dollar house and a family membership at the country club. I got a car out of the showroom at

16. My dad bought me a college education. I partied every day.

I had no interest in becoming a doctor. My brother, on the other hand, was the carbon copy. He always did and said the right thing. It was like always having two sets of footprints to walk in. The day I had to start calling my brother, Dr., was the worst day of my life.

I couldn't take it anymore. I was about 25 and stood up to my dad for the first time. I told him to leave me the _ _ _ _ alone. My mom always came to my rescue. My mom always understood my pain. After that day, my dad gave me the job as a supervisor over maintenance. It was cool. The day that changed my life happened to my dad. He died of a heart attack. For some reason, I was sad. I didn't feel like I lost my dad but my meal ticket.

My brother worked by my dad's side for five years before he died. I knew he would fire me, but surprisingly he didn't. We had a good run of no drama for years.

I met a customer and married her within one month. She reminded me of my mom. The next year my mom died. I have never felt so much pain in my life. I woke up every morning wanting to die. The other days I wondered why I'm still living.

Five or so years went by so fast. I was at work. My phone rang. My brother was in a car accident. I rushed over to the hospital. A car ran a red light and hit him on the driver's side. He was going to be out of work for a month. That was the best news in a while. I would be in charge of the building. My wife took care of the day-to-day. I finally got what I deserved. I was the boss.

This is where my life took a left turn. My brother came back from rehab, but he started taking oxycodone for pain. It only took about a month before he started writing his own prescriptions. He never married or had kids. He was a workaholic. I didn't know who he was. He was cool and calm. The oxycodone had him aggressive and loud. He spent the next few months after he returned missing appointments every day. My wife stepped in and hired another doctor to hold down the practice. My brother didn't care. I couldn't talk to him anymore.

It was a Sunday morning. Me and my wife were having breakfast at the kitchen table. The doorbell rang. I opened the door to an officer of the law. He asked my name. Then he wanted to come in. I had threatened this man to move his car out of the handicapped parking. I told the officer, "Before you get started, I told him several times to move." The officer said, "Your brother is dead." My knees buckled, and I hit the floor. He said he overdosed on oxycodone. It still doesn't feel any better. I feel lost. I feel worthless. I feel abandoned. Can you get me another beer? (I went to the store and bought him another beer.)

My problems started between me and my wife. I stopped going to the office and only wanted to sit at home. I was getting drunk every day. My wife now hired another Dr. The business was thriving. My wife came home with divorce papers, and I was furious. She called the cops, and they came and arrested me. I sat in jail for days.

I finally saw the judge. I was released and headed home. She had changed the locks. I walked down to the office. She called the cops again. She said I was trespassing on her property. Did you hear what I said? My wife always gave me papers to sign. She would tell me to sign because I was the boss. I didn't read anything. I signed a document wanting to divorce her. I signed the building over to her. I signed the house over to her. They were all notarized. I don't remember anyone else beginning there. During my drunken slumber, I was bamboozled.

My ex-wife gives me $100 every Monday. Today is Monday. Sometimes she doesn't come. I sit in this chair every Monday waiting. If you want to know the truth of the matter, I feel free. I no longer have to be what somebody else wants me to be. I don't feel any stress. I can make $20 a day *asking for help. I can get myself some beer, a sandwich, and a pack of cigarettes that last me three or four days. I have no worries. Everything happens for a reason. I am glad this happened to me. I hope your book turns out well. Thanks for the beer and cigarettes.*

I bring my brother's chair every Monday.

This book is one of the hardest things I've ever done in my life. I thought it would be easier with time. I try to take the emotions out of it. It cuts deeper and harder each time. I believed him when he said he was glad this life happened to him. The thing that always seems to come up is the agony of being homeless. I expected more trauma. I also expected escaped convicts on the run. I believe the stereotypes from the movies. Not because of being homeless but because of judging their past. I want to stop, but I have to keep going. I never can figure out their beginning or their end. I could never imagine feeling free because I was homeless.

Today is Saturday. All my days are great, but I find Saturdays the most fun. I get to spend time with my grandkids. I have a grandson who believes he is a baller. A baller is a person who is the best basketball player on the court. We get to the court early. There was a man shooting hoops by himself as we walked up. We went to the other end of the court. I know this guy hit 15 – 20 in a row without missing. He didn't even break a sweat. His shot was silk. Silk means when the ball goes through the hoop, it makes a popping sound. To further your education, you can watch basketball on tv. You can hear it in his voice, he was going to leave, and I told my grandson to shoot some free throws. I stopped the man.

Who do you play for?

I don't play for anyone. **I DIDN'T LISTEN.**

With a shot like that, what happened?

> *I will start from the beginning. I have always loved basketball. My mom bought me my first basketball when I was six years old, and I still have it in my room at my mom's house. I was always the best player on the court at age 6. I wore the number 23, and we all know who the number 23 is – Michael Jordan.*

> *I think I was in the 8th grade when my grades started slipping. I remember my mom telling me always to play the game with your mind but give your heart to God. I didn't listen. I had to sit out the first few games because of my grades. My mom went over to the school. She cried, telling them being a single parent is tough. I have*

no role models. I looked at her that day differently. I knew she was my mom, but why was my dad not around? On our ride home, I asked my mom about my dad. The subject never came up. She told me one night she had made a mistake. She went out on the town. She had too much to drink. Your father doesn't want to have anything to do with you because he is married to another lady. He denied you belonged to him.

What my mom said next jumpstarted me. She said, "Play basketball with your mind, not your heart. Your mind is your business. Take your feeling out of your business. Give your life to God. God will teach you how to feel good about your business. Your heart will have inner peace with God." I asked my mom to write it down. I didn't understand what it meant at the time. I looked at it every morning before I went to school. One day it made sense. I started talking to God. I woke every morning praying for God to make me a better basketball player. I asked him to get me to the pros. I still scored the most points on the team for high school. It's showtime. My praying had stopped over the summer. My mom worked a second job on Saturday and Sunday. I never knew that AAU basketball was so expensive. My mom hid that from me. I tried out for the team. Yes, you know it, I made varsity. I was playing with the seniors and juniors.

I was the youngest on the team. I didn't make the starting team. I would come in and take at least 5 – 6 shots. I would make no less than 4. Sometimes, I hit all 6. The coach wouldn't let me play more time that season. He told me I had to wait my turn. Coach told me I had time to be a star.

I wanted to be a star now. I have girls coming at me. I worked hard in the classroom and on my basketball skills. My mom told me she was proud of me. At the start of my senior year, I was in the news for being a top 10 player in the state. I was ready to shine. Our first game was a blowout. I scored 25 points. I didn't play in the 4th quarter; I sat on the bench.

This cheerleader for the other team was captivating. She tried to act like she didn't know I was staring at her. I walked over to her at the end of the game. I asked her for her phone number. She said she had a boyfriend. The next thing I know, I felt pain on the right side of my face. Her boyfriend played for the other team. We started fighting. The whole gym broke out in a brawl. I ended up getting suspended from school and the team for two weeks.

Here comes Mom, "I always told you to play basketball with your mind, not your heart." I didn't listen. I understand now, my senior year. If basketball were my business, don't mix business and pleasure. Those next two weeks changed *my life. I was hungry again. I got up every morning and came to this court right here. I shot hoops for hours.*

The second week was when I met Jessie. He was called Jessie James in the neighborhood. He asked me if I needed shoes or anything and said he saw me on tv. Now what happened next is what I wish I could take back. He gave me a beer. The rest of that week was spent hanging out with Jessie James.

I got back to school feeling different. My grades started slipping. Coach was now talking to my teachers. He kept me on the team. My shot was always nice. I would step on the court feeling like a baller. I had 20 scholarship offers. Three were at big schools. I wanted to be as close to Mom as I could. I took the offer an hour away. I had a roommate that was my teammate. He also thought he was a baller. We went to the gym every morning before classes.

The first season is football. Nobody knew who I was, and I couldn't wait until basketball season started. My roommate talked me into going to this party. They had a keg of beer, and I had never seen a keg before. I was feeling very good. I saw this young lady. I walked up to her. I said, "I'm your future husband."

She said, "I have a boyfriend."

I didn't care and said, "It's loud in here; let's go outside."

We get outside. We begin to talk. You already know what happened next. Yes, I felt a hit on my arm, and it was a bullet. Her boyfriend shot me. The sad part is no one snitched. I still, to this day, don't know the name of the person who shot me. I was shot in my arm right here.

When I got back home, I started getting disability checks for PTSD. My arm has healed, but that night will never go away. I play the what-if game every day in my mind. I love watching basketball on tv. It comes with a price to pay in my mind. I get a disability check first of the month. I make sure I take care of my mom. She won't let me drink beer in her house. I run the streets for about 2 or 3 weeks. Most times, until my money runs out. I also beg for money. I sleep outside, at the shelter, or in a portable toilet.

I didn't listen; I didn't listen, I didn't listen.

My mom told me my talent is because of my heart work, but peace comes from God. (heart work means passion) I didn't listen. You can mention my name in your book if you like. I think your son is ready to go. I have to get home before Mom gets off work.

Basketball dreams left behind.

The funny thing is when my grandson got in the car, I looked at him. His story could be the same path my grandson could be on. I went back to that park every Saturday for two months. He finally showed up. I gave him my book, MY TRUTH - 10 DAYS, 10 WORDS, and the journal that goes with it. I signed it to a person who inspired me to continue to write. We shot some hoops. He worked on my grandson's shot. I don't know how his story ends. It has only just begun.

Isaiah 32:18 ESV

"My people will abide in a peaceful habitation, in secure dwellings, and in quiet resting places."

Wake me up when it is over.

About the Author

Dwight Hairston Currence resides in Charlotte, North Carolina. He loves the Lord and strives daily to inspire others to be confident in who they are. Dwight wants everyone to understand how wonderful life can be when you love God first and learn to let Him direct your life.

Photo credits, including the author's photo, go to:

Doreen Tyrelle, This is Photography!
Charlotte, NC

Books by Author

My Truth: 10 Days 10 Words (Paperback)
ISBN 979-8-9871031-0-4

My Truth: 10 Days 10 Words (Kindle)
ISBN 979-8-9871031-2-8

My Truth Journal
ISBN 979-8-9871031-1-1 (Paperback)

Seven Deadly Sins & Heavenly Virtues
ISBN 979-8-9871031-3-5 (Paperback)

Seven Deadly Sins & Heavenly Virtues
ISBN 979-8-9871031-5-9 (Kindle)

www.ingramcontent.com/pod-product-compliance
Lightning Source LLC
Chambersburg PA
CBHW060258030426
42335CB00014B/1758